Living Through The Grief

Memories of Mother

Leigh Ann Pearson

Endorsements

Leigh Ann and I grew up together on Leslie Street in the big city of Stuttgart, AR. We walked to and from grade school and stayed together after school. We had strict rules about what to and not to do, but her sweet mother always had our snacks waiting on us, even though she was working. She was a very beautiful and sweet woman, but most importantly a Godly woman! She made our young lives better, such fun, what great memories I have!

Melanie Ferguson
Stuttgart, Arkansas

Growing up in the 70's in a small-town Arkansas neighborhood was like having family for blocks and blocks. We became friends with nearby neighbors and spent our days going back and forth from house to house. After reading Leigh Ann's manuscript, I realized how little I knew about what was happening in my childhood. Leigh Ann's mother was always smiling and welcoming whenever I came to their house. She always made me feel at home and a part of the family. I remember only happy times when I would visit their home. I can completely understand the enormous hole left in Leigh Ann's heart at the loss of her sweet mother.

Laurie Ruff Timmons; Springdale, Arkansas

LIVING THROUGH THE GRIEF

Leigh Ann Pearson's "Living Through the Grief ~ Memories of Mother" captures the emotional complexity of loss in a way that is both deeply personal and universally relatable. Her raw and open relationship with God throughout her grieving process is something I found deeply comforting. As I processed my own grief, the loss of my 22-year-old nephew Kalel Jackson in 2023, this book brought me peace and clarity in ways I didn't expect. Leigh Ann's vulnerability allows readers to see that it's okay to be angry, ask God the difficult questions, and to sit with the unanswered "why's" that often haunt us. Her words reminded me that God's love doesn't leave us, even when we feel lost in sorrow.

Leigh Ann's story is a powerful testament to the hope that can be found even in the midst of pain. I highly recommend this book for anyone who is walking through grief and looking for healing.

~ Amika Coleman
Real Estate Broker/Owner
Southern California

Foreword

I have known Leigh Ann Hagaman Pearson for over 60 years. We met in the pre-school Sunday School Department at First Baptist Church in Stuttgart, AR. I don't have a memory of that first meeting, she was just always a parat of my life. What drew us together and bonded us as sister at that young age? I dont know, except God had a plan and arranged for us to be together. We hshared the typical growing up experiences of the 60's-70's in a small rural southern town. School, music, boys, slumber parties, birthday parties, summertime activities and eventually part time jobs (we both worked in jewelry stores) were our lives durimg those growing up years. We lived across town fro eachother but Leigh Ann's Mother, AKA Mamma H, worked at West Department Store in the shoe department which was close to our school. Every day when we were in Jr. High we walked from school to the store. Mamma H took her dinner break at 4:00 PM to take Leigh Ann home from school and drop me off at my house. I don't remember the discussions we had during those rides home only that there was a lot of smiles and laughter and that we all three sat in the front seat! No seat belt laws in those days! Our extra-curricular activities centered around the Church; Sunday school, youth group, choir trips, church camp, etc. It wasn't until I was an adult that I realized Leigh Ann's Mother musth have done without many personal wants and needs so that Leigh Ann could have these life changing opportunities. A few of my favorite memories about Mrs. Frances Hagaman, the one whose life inpsired Leigh Ann to write this book: She had a beautiful Southern drawl from her native state of Alabama and her words were always delived with a smile and word of encouragement. Her hair always look immaculate. Ladies that worked outside the home in those days would o to the Beauty Shop to get their hair shampooed and set and somehow it lasted beautifully for a week! Her nails were always painted red and manicured beautifully. This small pleasure was not out of vanity but to put her best self forward in the work place and community AND to model to her young daughter no matter what your circumstances, take care of your temple. And lastly, she always wore red lipstick. It was beautiful with her dark hair. Red lipstick is and has always been my favorite, I'm sure due to that early imprinting!

Leigh Ann and I were inseparable and were definitely each other's "secret keeper, encourager and rock of protection". Leigh Ann's family lived in a big old house with hight ceilings, wood floors and rooms that flowed from one to the next. I still love old houses probably because of the many happy hours spent in the Hagaman home. Leigh Ann will describe her home from her perspective in the book. A strong reminder that we shouldn't assume what goes on behind closed doors. We were living our best life in small town America. We shared AL-MOST everything. A well-kept secret that was hidden deep inside the hear of this home for many years even to Leigh Ann was one thing that we didn't share, Leigh Ann's Father was an alcoholic. As much time as I spent in that home, I never knew this. And if my parents knew, it was never mentioned. I realize now just how much of a burden Mamma

H shouldered alone to make sure her home was a peaceful and loving place for Leigh Ann and her friends.

After High School graduation, we attended Southern Baptist College, now Williams Baptist University together. Our freshman year of college Leigh Ann's homelife changed drastically. By age 25 both of her parents were gone. So yea, grief is something Leigh Ann knows about firsst hand and writes about truthfully from her heart. She has "livved with grief" for most of her life.

When I received the "Living Through The Grief" manuscript, I did not expect it to be something that I could use since I haven't experienced a loss of this magnitude. But what I found as I read through it is a great tool for processing grief of any kind, loss due to death, loss of relationships or unprocessed feelings that may keep us from moving forward. We all have loss and sometimes it's an unfair loss like described in this book. But by reading the scriptures, prayer, journaling and the never-ending love of our Heavenly Father we can live life and live it ABUNDANTLY (beyond what we can imagine).

I hope you will read and really use this book as Leigh Ann walks us through some thoughts that may seem too painful to put onto paper and process. It took Leigh Ann 45 years to come to the point of sharing such raw and painful memories. Grief is hard and many times all consuming. Let this be your first step toward healing and living the life God created for you. Also consider friends and family that have or are experiencing grief. Let this little book be your way to show them how much you care about their healing.

I think you're going to love this book as much as I did!

Paulette Hill
Mt Home, Arkansas

"The thief (grief, sadness, anger, denial, depression, hate, resentment) comes only to steal, kill and destroy. I (Jesus) came that you may have life and have it ABUNDANTLY (prosper, generously, lavishly, richly, FREELY, magnificently, peacefully)"John 10:10

PPT (Paulette's Personal Translation)

Contents

Acknowledgements

I want to thank my PaPa for asking me to write, covering me with His patience over the years as He waited for me to be obedient and tackle the unknown, walk by faith, and become an Author. I'm so humbled and excited to write as He talks with me. I'm having the time of my life on this adventure with my Heavenly Father. I especially want to thank Him for placing a question on Amika's heart for me. Thank You, PaPa!!

Amika ~ There are no words to express my thanks! I'm so grateful to Jesus that He chose you to trust with the question that would lead to my complete healing of grief. You are His GateKeeper! You never gave up asking and continued until I finally gave in, and for that, I'm forever grateful to you. I love you.

To my amazing husband, Steven how can I even begin to express how much your prayers, encouragement, and support mean to me? You accepted this wonderful world of writing books right alongside me. You have spent countless hours learning how to work programs, and then teaching me. You have designed two beautiful prayer rooms for me to write in. You are beyond patient, kind, generous, and loving as you walked out every step of this self-publishing adventure with me. You prayed through each letter, word, scripture, punctuation, and more. I love you.

I am so blessed to have my four young adult children, Brooks, Krista, Kyle, and Bilal who always encourage and cheer me on through every book. I value your gifts of encouragement and treasure them in my heart! I love ya'll.

My beautiful granddaughter, River brings me joy and unconditional love, fueling my heart to be a better LaLa for her. She has no idea because she is only 2 years old, but she propels me into my PaPa's arms daily. Thank you, Rivy ~ I love you.

My beautiful spiritual daughter and sons, Lykia, Nash, and Veasna are a source of love and encouragement. Although we live in different countries, we are closer than when we first met. I love ya'll.

To my incredibly talented daughter, Krista who conquered the world of formatting and designing book covers! She is 100% a natural in this realm and does it with such ease. Her eye for perfection, beauty, and wisdom comes straight from PaPa's Throne Room. Her palate of colors and how to intertwine them is impeccable! The programs for writing/formatting/cover designs were such a HUGE hurdle for me to jump over. I had cried buckets and just given up when she offered to help me. Her patience as she became my teacher is something that I will cherish for the rest of my life. I will forever have the beautiful portrait of us sitting in front of my computer, working on my projects. I love you more than all the stars in the sky!

I would be lost without my Dream Team of prayer warriors. You stay close to me and pray for me, each book, and future readers. Your unselfish partnership with me is stamped on every page of my books. With such a grateful heart, I wish to thank: Nancy, Paulette, Wendy, George, Alcira, Toni, Tammy, Rita, Diana, Sothea, Vesna, Nash, Avis, and Karina. I love each one of you more than words can express.

I also have a sweet circle of dear friends and family who constantly encourage and pray for my books. However, to list them all would develop a book itself. So to each of you ~ I want to thank you for your support, encouragement, patience, and love. I love each one of you dearly!

Preface

As I share my heart about my mother with you, I will also talk about my PaPa. I want to explain that my PaPa is my name for The One True God. Most people call Him Heavenly Father, Daddy, or Dad. He and I had a talk years ago when I wanted to strengthen our relationship and grow closer to Him. At that time, I asked Him if I could call Him PaPa and He said yes.

My mother and I were very close and in my opinion, she was the very best mother. She was fun, loved to laugh, loved to be silly, loved road trips & loved Jesus. She journaled on scrap pieces of paper, which I'd find on our kitchen table or tucked away on the shelf. Mother was the perfect reflection of Jesus and she lived to bring Him glory. I could see the reflection of Jesus in her shining bright. She loved to listen to Billy Graham's sermons and had some of his books. She was faithful in our Southern Baptist Church and made sure I was active in our Youth Group. She led me to accept Jesus as my personal Lord and Savior when I was 9 years old.

Life was tough, my daddy was an alcoholic and drank up most of our money. We lived in a house that was 100 years old and had rotten areas in many rooms, including a large hole in the roof over the bathtub. Yet our home was clean and full of love. Mother worked for West Brothers and later in life, she began working for Belk's, which are retail stores where she was on her feet all day. She never complained about being tired or that her feet hurt. She always wore a smile. I will never forget her response when I told her that I hated my daddy. She hugged me and told me to hate what he did and not to hate him! His alcohol addiction was hard to live through, but it brought me so much closer to Jesus, and for that, I'm forever grateful!

Mother went to be with Jesus on 4/7/79. This was the saddest day of my life! This book is a reflection of my mother's love for her family, friends, and her love for Jesus. It is also my memories of walking through my grief. I hope it will be helpful to you as you walk through your grief.

Much Love,
Leigh Ann
xoxo

Psalm 89:1 "I will sing of the Lord's great love forever; with my mouth I will make your faithfulness known through all generations."

Meet the Hagaman Family

♥

My mother is Frances Juanita Gibson Hagaman, born on November 15, 1920. She married my daddy, Francis King (Sam) Hagaman on September 14, 1940 (he was born on October 18, 1916). They moved from Alabama to Arkansas into our house at 409 S. Leslie Street when I was 2 years old. They had 3 children: Jan, Chuck, and Leigh Ann. Jan and Chuck are two years apart, while I joined the family 13 years after Chuck was born. I must share that it's fun being the baby of the family. I lived a carefree life for the most part and was a typical kid growing up in the 60s. For those younger than me, living in the South in the 60's meant you never had to lock your house or car doors! Even during Christmas when there are gifts under the tree! Mother protected me from the alcohol darkness that my daddy suffered for as long as she could, which was until I became a teenager. He didn't abuse any of us, he just stole our money (including my lunch money) so he could drink. His life is yet another story for another time, I just wanted to give you a little bit about him, so you can understand my mother better.

Mother loved to play the piano and sing when I was little. My brother shared that she even sang in the church choir. But when I came along she went to work and had to give up singing in the choir. She had the most beautiful first sopranino voice! I'm sure she is singing beautiful songs to Jesus right now! Her days off were Sunday and Tuesday for all of my life. I'm so sad now as an adult to look at her working career because she did not get the opportunity to enjoy two days off in a row like I did. Neither did she have the chance to retire from work. Yet, she never complained and was filled with such joy from PaPa! After church each Sunday, she and I would always take a short road trip through the country just outside of Stuttgart. Many times she would let me invite a friend to join us. She enjoyed picking Catail stalks along the roadside and adding them to her bouquet from her garden. We had fun talks and tons of laughs. I'm sure this is why I have always loved to take road trips with my husband. On Tuesday, she would go to the hair salon and then spend hours in the laundromat doing our laundry. I'm sure she utilized this time on PaPa's lap too. She would find time to work in her flower garden weekly. She had the most beautiful garden and it came so effortlessly to her. I think she found peace in the garden and I'm sure she had deep conversations with PaPa while she tended to it.

Mother would get up early each day, get a cup of coffee, and spend time alone with PaPa. She didn't own a notebook or journal, so she'd write on scratch paper. I'd find her notes to PaPa tucked away throughout the house. I must get my love for journaling from her. She lived a life that reflected Jesus so well and taught me so many life lessons. I can remember her saving up money to buy some paint for our living room. She and I went to Sears to pick up the paint, and as we put it into our car, she noticed they had accidentally given us one can too many. She immediately returned it to the clerk. This moment never left me, because she had such a close relationship with our Heavenly Father that she always wanted to do what was right, even if no one was watching.

She was the kind of individual whom you would have liked if you had the opportunity to meet. She was so filled with the joy of the Lord, that you would never think she had any difficult moments, let alone a hard life. The financial struggles that tried to choke her, keeping me safe and unaware of daddy's drinking problem, living in a house that was falling apart, and the list goes on. By this time, Jan had gotten married and moved out of the house while Chuck had moved out of town to attend college. so it was just Mother, Daddy, and me left in the house.

Mother was my encourager and my rock growing up. Her love was so tangible and comforting. I miss her very much.

Joshua 1:9 "Have I not commanded you? Be strong and courageous. Do not be terrified; do not be discouraged, for the Lord your God will be with you wherever you go."

REFLECTING PAGE

- Take a moment to list the things that you took away from my story. Maybe pieces of our family puzzle remind you of your family or close friends.

_____

_____

_____

- **Who is your encourager?**

_____

- **Who is your rock of protection?**

_____

- **Who makes you laugh the most?**

_____

- **Who is your secret keeper?**

_____

- **What are your hobbies?**

_____

- **Are you an encourager?**

_____

- **Are you a rock of protection?**

- **Do you make someone laugh?**

- **Do you keep secrets for someone?**

- **Can your hobbies be used to bless others?**

If you cannot answer the questions and list the name of the individual(s), please take a few minutes and invite the Holy Spirit to help you. Maybe this is the time to make positive changes within your family and let it start with YOU! You can be the **Encourager ~ Rock ~ Funny ~ Secret Keeper.** You have a special and valuable place to hold within your family tree.

Proverbs 31:15-31

"[15] Even in the night season she arises and sets food on the table for hungry ones in her house and for others. [16] She sets her heart upon a nation and takes it as her own, carrying it within her. She labors there to plant the living vines. [17] She wraps herself in strength, might, and power in all her works. [18] She tastes and experiences a better substance, and her shining light will not be extinguished, no matter how dark the night. [19]She stretches out her hands to help the needy and she lays hold of the wheels of government. [20] She is known by her extravagant generosity to the poor, for she always reaches out her hands to those in need. [21] She is not afraid of tribulation, for all her household is covered in the dual garments of righteousness and grace. [22] Her clothing is beautifully knit together – a purple gown of exquisite linen. [23] Her husband is famous and admired by all, sitting as the venerable judge of his people. [24] Even her works of righteousness she does for the benefit of her enemies. [25] Bold power and glorious majesty are wrapped around her as she laughs with joy over the latter days. [26] Her teachings are filled with wisdom and kindness as loving instruction pours from her lips. [27] She watches over the ways of her household and meets every need they have. [28] Her sons and daughters arise in one accord to extol her virtues, and her husband arises to speak of her in glowing terms. [29] There are many valiant and noble ones, but you have ascended above them all! [30] Charm can be misleading, and beauty is vain and so quickly fades, but this virtuous woman lives in the wonder, awe, and fear of the Lord. She will be praised throughout eternity. [31] So go ahead and give her the credit that is due, for she has become a radiant woman, and all her loving works of righteousness deserve to be admired at the gateways of every city!"

(TPT, The Passion Translation Bible)

Singing for Jesus

♥

A s a child, I sat next to my mother in church every Sunday. I loved to hear her sing to Jesus. She had the most beautiful voice and it gently lifted my heart. I wanted to sing like Mother with all of my heart. I'm happy to share that Jesus gave me her voice and I love to sing for Him also. I believe singing is more than sitting with the choir, or pew on Sunday. It's an action of worship to our Lord and Savior. It's our heartfelt melody of love that we share with Him. It's our symphony of praise and adoration to the one true God! When you feel this in your heart, you know that you can't sing a beautiful song one minute and then yell at your loved ones the next. While it's a big piece of worship, what we do with the remainder of our time is just as important. We are still "singing" with our hearts as we do life!

My mother did this with excellence! As I mentioned, life was hard for her and not many folks knew it. Unfortunately, alcohol kept my daddy in bed most of the time. He did work until I was in Jr High when he was injured, due to him drinking on the job. This caused him to retire early. Now mother was the only source of income for our family. I was blessed to babysit for a lot of people in our church and that was my source of income.

Unfortunately, my Grandmother (Daddy's mother) was not kind to my mother. She treated her as if she hated her instead of valuing the wonderful daughter-in-law that she was. Grandmother was retired but refused to babysit me when mother went back to work. So Mother had to pay our neighbor's sweet daughter, Kay to babysit me after school. Grandmother would call the house and when we answered she would say "Is Sam there?". There was never a "hello" or "how are you" to anyone else. I'm not sharing this to bash my Grandmother but to honestly paint the full picture of my mother's life. You see, mother never once spoke ill towards my Grandmother. She honored her every chance she got. Even when I would ask why she was so mean, Mother would respond with Grandmother's positive attributes.

Mother never raised her voice or spoke ugly towards my daddy either. I would tell her that I "hated him" and she would respond, "Don't hate him, hate what he does". I never saw her be jealous of others either. She was content because she had such joy from the Lord. It was evident that His JOY was deep within her soul. I only saw His Joy, love, and compassion displayed by my mother. She was amazing! So in my heart, she was constantly singing for Jesus and her life displayed a *beautiful symphony of love* and devotion for Him. Now I do want you to know that Mother was not perfect, but seriously through my eyes, she was. As I'm sharing my heart with you, the Holy Spirit is gently convicting me in the areas where I need to make better choices. So after 45 years of being unable to see, hug, or talk with my mother, she is still teaching me!

Matthew 18:19 "Again, I give you an eternal truth: If two of you agree to ask God for something in **a symphony of prayer**, my heavenly Father will do it for you." **(TPT, The Passion Translation)**

REFLECTING PAGE

- Take a moment to list the things that you took away from my story. Maybe pieces of our family puzzle remind you of your family or close friends.

_____

_____

_____

- I'm talking to myself, as I talk with you ~ let's slow down and think before we say a word. Let's make sure our words come from our hearts and not out of frustration, jealousy, or anger. Even if we have a reason not to like someone, let's be encouraged to find a reason.

- Let's give the Holy Spirit a moment to bring any situation where our words were hurtful to our minds.

  ○ What did the Holy Spirit tell you?

  _____

  ○ Do you need to apologize to anyone?

  _____

  ○ Have you missed an opportunity to encourage someone?

  _____

    • It's not too late, give them a call today.

Psalm 98:5

"Sing your melody of praise to the Lord and make music like never before!" (TPT, The Passion Translation Bible)

Loving the Grands

♥

The legacy of Frances J. Gibson Hagaman is her children, the sweet grandchildren, great-grandchildren, and great-great-grandson she knew as well as those born after her death. Both Jan and Chuck's children were blessed to know their Grandmother very well. They spent a lot of time with her and it truly warms my heart to think back on the memories of the time they had together. Unfortunately, she passed away before my daughters were born, which breaks my heart; but they know her through my memories and pictures.

Each one of us has a legacy. I want you to take a few minutes and jot down your legacy. If you don't have children, you might have nieces and nephews or you have close friends and their children are "yours" too. Any way you look at it, you are leaving a legacy for others! I want to encourage you to make a note of what you want your loved ones to learn from you and remember about you. I promise you, that YOU are a valued piece of your family! You are a teacher, mentor, sister, brother, mother, father, aunt, uncle, cousin, and friend to so many people in your world! I challenge you to make a note of the most important things (not anything tangible) that you want to leave for each of your own loved ones when you pass away.

As you are doing this, I realize you might not know Jesus as your own personal Lord & Savior. Let's take a moment for you to meet Jesus! He left a legacy of love for all of us, a legacy of salvation. If you feel Him tugging on your heart, please take this moment to repent of your sins & ask Jesus to come into your life. He will come into your heart **IMMEDIATELY**. This is a promise that He gave us in the Bible, found in **John 3:16** "For God so loved the world that he gave his one and only son, that whoever believes in him shall not perish but have eternal life." Welcome to the Family of God dear friend! Please share this great news with someone. I also want to encourage you to find a church where you can learn more about Jesus.

So let's meet them in birth order:

Jan's children
- Terri

- Jim

- Nancy

- Bryan

- Hannah

    ○ **Grandchildren**

      - Samantha

      - Cache

- Bryana

- Maraye

- Price

  ○ **Great Grand**

    - Tate

Chuck's children
- Andy

- Rex

- Brooks

  ○ **Grandchild**

    - West

Leigh Ann's children
- Brooks

- Krista

  ○ **Grandchildren**

    - River

    - River's brother, Khalil Kai is due Jan 2025

My Mother has a legacy of 22 people at the time that I'm writing this book. That's a lot of people for one person to love and influence. That's a lot of wonderful memories. Our family tree's strongest branches are the ones that my mother watered, pruned, and prayed over. I hope this will help you view your family tree in a new way. Because you have so much value, worth, and love to share with your loved ones. Whether your family is small or large isn't the question at hand. The question is are you building a strong legacy for your loved ones? Will your family tree be strong because of you and your faith in Jesus? Are you taking the steps to build a strong family tree? The lives of your loved ones depend upon it. I want to encourage you to leave beautiful blossoms with strong branches, thick with the most amazing leaves on your family tree.

Proverbs 13:22 "A good man leaves an inheritance for his children's children, but a sinner's wealth is stored up for the righteous."

REFLECTING PAGE

- *List or draw your family tree below. Trust me, it's fun to see everyone listed together. If I were an artist, I would have drawn a beautiful magnolia tree and listed my family on the blossoms.*

- *Psalm 122:8*

"I intercede for the sake of my family and friends who dwell there, that they may all live in peace." (TPT, The Passion Translation Bible)

What Would the Neighbors Say?

♥

My mother had a strong Alabama accent, so do your best to say "What would the neighbors say?" in your best deep southern drawl. lol

After Chuck graduated from college, he begged his mother to divorce Daddy, and he promised to provide financially for his mother and me. She could not see divorce as an option, because she knew that PaPa hated divorce. Fast forward many years later and as a teenager, I begged her to divorce Daddy too. This time her response was "What would the neighbors say"? As a true Southern woman, she was brought up to always think about what others thought of her. Because this question ended both of our conversations with her about this subject matter, I can only speculate that her foundational reason was that she would not do something that her Heavenly Father hated.

They were married for almost 39 years. I'm sure in the early stages of their life together, they were very much in love and happy. That's the thing with taking just one sip of alcohol, you just never know if you will become addicted to it or not. Unfortunately, daddy was the one who fought this addiction most of his life. I would like to share that Daddy became sober a few years after Mother's death. I'm so happy that he found sobriety, just sorry that it took so long.

My mother put herself last all of the time. As I'm writing this book, I hear the Holy Spirit asking me to make healthier choices when eating, add exercising regularly into my life, continue my daily quiet times with PaPa, and stay plugged into our church are all ways that I can show my family that I love them. This is huge for me because everything tastes better if it's deep-fried. lol Honestly, I believe that mother saw herself as a walking and talking advertisement for Jesus.

Ephesians 1:19 "I pray that you will continually experience the immeasurable greatness of God's power made available to you through faith. ***Then your lives will be an advertisement of this immense power as it works through you!*** This is the mighty power [20]that was released when God raised Christ from the dead and exalted him to the place of highest honor and supreme authority in the heavenly realm! **(TPT; The Passion Translation Bible)**

REFLECTING PAGE

- Take a moment to list the things that you took away from my story.

_____

_____

_____

- Instead of being concerned about what the neighbors would say, how about we concentrate on what Jesus would say? What are your thoughts?

_____

_____

_____

- In what ways is your life a walking advertisement for Jesus?

_____

_____

_____

- What changes are you willing to make to be a better advertisement for Jesus?

_____

_____

_____

A Tender Heart

♥

M other had such a tender heart for everyone. A tender heart allows us to see the best in others. A tender heart always thinks of the good in others, even when they are covered in mud. It is when we have a tender heart, that the Holy Spirit can use us to be a blessing. Let's face it, we hear Him when our hearts are tender and willing to be utilized for His glory.

Mother always encouraged me to look at the positive attributes that people had, rather than their faults. Each time I pointed out a negative view of someone, she would cover it with a positive one. Looking back on her life, it seems like the negative outweighed the positive. Yet her heart was filled with the joy that only the Holy Spirit can give us. Mother rejoiced and praised PaPa before she saw the outcome or answer to her prayers. She went to Heaven without seeing many of her prayers fulfilled, yet she chose JOY. His joy is contagious too! I believe everyone wants to be filled with His joy. Are you a joy shaker for the Lord like my mother was? It's not too late, you can ask the Lord to help you be His joy shaker and start today. A joy shaker is similar to sprinkling colorful sprinkles onto cupcakes. I encourage you to sprinkle His joy with each step you take!

Psalm 32:10 -11 "Many are the woes of the wicked, but the Lord's unfailing love surrounds the man who trusts in him. [11] Rejoice in the Lord and be glad, you righteous; sing, all you who are upright in heart!"

REFLECTING PAGE

- Take a moment to list the things that you took away from my story. Did anything hit home with you?

_____

_____

_____

- So I want you to take a moment and look inward at your heart. Do you have a tender heart?

_____

- What makes your heart tender?

_____

_____

_____

- What would make your heart even more tender?

_____

_____

_____

- I want to encourage you to take a moment and talk with the Holy Spirit about your heart. Ask Him to take a closer look at your heart. Ask Him to convict you if you have any sin hanging out inside that you might not even be aware of. Give Him a few minutes to talk with you before you move on.

_____

_____

_____

Preparing for Death

♥

I honestly believe that Mother knew she was gonna die, her spiritual life was in great shape, and she wanted to ensure I was taken care of, and that I had money to live on after her death. She took out a life insurance policy that was very difficult for her to purchase because it was expensive but she did this months maybe even a year before her first visit to the physician. After Mother passed away, Jan took me around town and I paid all of Mother's bills including her funeral with this money.

You see on my 19th birthday, she had exploratory surgery which is when they located ovarian cancer. Mother was at stage 3. There are 4 stages to ovarian cancer. There are no words to express the deep emotional level of sadness that overcame me when the physician gave us this news. When I was at my mother's bedside, I was happy and hopeful. I remember telling her that if John Wayne could fight cancer, she could too. I watched my mother lose so much weight and look very frail. She was unable to lift a glass of water. My heart broke into millions of pieces, yet we all prayed for her miracle. We believed and prayed for two months until she passed away.

At 19 years of age, I loved Jesus and knew that I was saved. But I did not have an intimate relationship with Him until I was in my mid-50s. I'm so grateful that the Holy Spirit never gives up on us! By this stage in my life, I worked for our church and began to take classes, upon classes to learn more about our Heavenly Father, Jesus, and the Holy Spirit. As I grew in Him, I was able to hear His voice. In my quiet times, He would talk to me and then He began talking with me all day and night. Life was great!

Romans 6:23 "For the wages of sin is death, but the gift of God is eternal life in Christ Jesus our Lord."

REFLECTING PAGE

- Take a moment to list the things that you took away from my story. Did anything hit home with you?

_____

_____

- Do you know Jesus as your personal Lord and Savior?

_____

- If not, please pause here and ask Him to forgive you of your sins, tell Him that you believe He is God, and come into your life now. He will come into your heart immediately.

_____

- Share your decision for Jesus with others today.

_____

- Congratulations and welcome to the Family of God!!!

- If you already knew Him ~ please join me in praying for others to come to know Him. List the first people who come into your mind who don't know Jesus yet:

_____

_____

_____

April 7th, 1979

♥

This date is the darkest day that I've ever experienced in my life. It is the day that PaPa called my mother HOME with Him. While I'm most grateful that she is now with Jesus and that I will see her again as we worship PaPa in person throughout all of eternity. I do miss her with all of my heart. I am now 64 years old and it has been 45 years since my mother passed away. I've lived without her in my life longer than I had her in my life. I can live my regular day-to-day life, but holidays are sprinkled with moments that are still difficult and Mother's Day is always bitter/sweet. My daughters spend time with me and celebrate with me, which fills my heart with joy, in the quietness of that holiday my heart always thanks Jesus for my Mother. When Brooks and Krista were born my heart hurt because they would not have the opportunity to know and love her. Although because both of my daughters have Jesus as their own personal Lord and Savior, they of course will meet her one day in Heaven. Until that day, I've shared memories and pictures of my mother with the girls. So I'm sure they feel as if they know her. Fun fact ~ Brooks and Krista know her as Granny Frances, which is what she wanted to be called.

To be completely honest, shortly after my mother passed away, I wanted to die. Although I never tried to take my life, I went out into my sister's field and cried my eyes out, as I did, I told Jesus that I wanted to die too! I didn't want to live one more minute without my mother. Then I asked Him why He had taken my mother first. Why didn't He take my daddy? After all, my mother was living for Jesus and my daddy was living for the next drink! I was such a broken vessel at that moment. Right after I asked Him these questions my sweet niece, Terri found me, put her arms around me, and encouraged me. Although I can't recall what Terri said to me at all, PaPa was with us in that moment and the desire to die was gone. Terri and I went into the house and life became a new normal for me without my mother.

Ten years after Mother passed away, I was missing her voice so much. I remember sitting in my car in the driveway trying to catch my breath and stop crying, telling PaPa I wished I could hear her voice just one more time. When I went into the house, I began looking for something (I can't remember what I needed), but what I found was straight from my PaPa's Throne Room! It was a cassette tape. Not just any cassette tape, when I popped it into the player I heard my mother talking to me! She says "Leigh Ann, you'd better watch that tom cat of yours" and that was the only thing she said. Needless to say, my tears started flowing again, but this time with such joy! PaPa answered my prayer and I have that cassette tape in a very safe spot. Years have passed and we no longer had a cassette player. My wonderful husband surprised me by purchasing a cassette player. So now I can listen to my mother's beautiful voice anytime I want to.

PaPa cares about the things we care about!

Psalm 56:8 "You've kept track of all my wandering and my weeping. You've stored my many tears in your bottle – not one will be lost. For they are all recorded in your book of remembrance." **(TPT, The Passion Translation Bible)**

REFLECTING PAGE

- Take a moment to list the things that you took away from my story. Did anything hit home with you?

_____

_____

_____

- Are there any dates in time that stand out to you, as April 7, 1979, does for me? Maybe it wasn't a death, but a trauma nonetheless. Anything that hurts you, hurts your Heavenly Father's heart too.

_____

_____

_____

- Is there anything that you want to give to Jesus?

_____

_____

_____

Life Without Mother

♥

The birth of Brooks and Krista eased the pain of living without my mother. I can't explain it, but they did ease my pain of missing her so much. Oh grant it I do have my moments when all of a sudden I'll miss her deeply and fight the tears. I believe having her pictures around my home and sharing her stories with my daughters has helped with my healing to be honest.

I also believe that the 19 years I had her in my life, she taught me the most important lesson. Which is to love the Lord with all of my heart and trust Him completely. She not only verbally talked with me about His love and trust, but she lived a life full of love, and adoration, and trusted Him completely herself.

Mother's favorite Bible verses

- **Psalm 23**

  - "The Lord is my shepherd, I shall not be in want. [2]He
    makes me lie down in green pastures, he leads me beside
    quiet waters,[3]he restores my soul. He guides me in paths
    of righteousness for his name's sake. [4]Even though I walk
    through the valley of the shadow of death, I will fear
    no evil, for you are with me, your rod and your staff,
    they comfort me.[5]You prepare a table before me in the
    presence of my enemies. You anoint my head with oil;
    my cup overflows. [6]Surely goodness and love will follow
    me all the days of my life, and I will dwell in the house of
    the Lord forever."

- **Romans 8:28**

  - "And we know that in all things God works for the good
    of those who love him, who have been called according
    to his purpose."

- **Philippians 4:13**

  - "I can do everything through him who gives me
    strength."

- **Isaiah 26:3**

  - "You will keep in perfect peace him whose mind is stead-
    fast, because he trusts in you."

REFLECTING PAGE

- Take a moment to list the things that you took away from my story. Did anything hit home with you?

_____

_____

_____

- List your favorite Bible verses:

_____

_____

_____

- Now jot down why each verse is a favorite. What makes this verse REAL and powerful to you?

_____

_____

_____

- One of my favorite Bible verses:

Ephesians 3:20 "Never *doubt* God's mighty power to work in you and accomplish all this. He will achieve infinitely more than your greatest request, your most unbelievable dream and exceed your wildest imagination! He will outdo them all, for his miraculous power constantly energizes you." **(TPT, The Passion Translation Bible)**

So dream BIGGER, my friend, dream BIGGER!

Amika's Question

♥

The pathway that led to my grief healing began the day I met Amika. Amika and I worked together at our church for many years. From day one, our hearts were knitted together and we became sisters. One day in 2013, Amika asked me a strange question. She asked, "Were you mad at your mother for dying?". My response was to throw back my head and laugh hard, as I replied, "That's the dumbest question I've ever heard", "She didn't take her life, she died from ovarian cancer". When I asked why she would ask such a dumb question, her sweet reply was "God told me to ask you". I thought this was a strange question and quickly dismissed it.

Well, let me tell you, Amika asked me this same question for several weeks, maybe even a month. I responded in the same manner every time she asked me. Amika was always gentle with me and very kind. I, on the other hand, would laugh at her question and judge it harshly. Until the last time she presented this same question, I shared that she was on my last nerve and that I would talk with PaPa about it, just to get her to quit asking me! As you can imagine, she smiled and sweetly said "ok, good". That's one of the things I love about Amika, is that we can talk about PaPa and what He is doing in our lives. She was and is a safe place for me.

The next morning in my quiet time, I asked PaPa what was going on with Amika's question. In His tender, loving, compassionate voice, He told me that I had not been mad at my mother for dying. "GREAT! I can hardly wait to tell Amika!" was my reply; "But wait sweetheart," PaPa said. "My dear, you were mad at ME." He replied. My heart fell at this moment! WHAT! I have been mad at my PaPa for 34 years!!! Tears began to fall down my cheeks as I fell to the floor and cried. I could not believe that I had been carrying this anger towards my PaPa, the one who knows me best and loves me the most! I repented for my sin of anger and asked Him to forgive me. Which of course He did immediately! I felt this rush of His never-ending love filling me up as His arms hugged me. It was such a powerful moment in my life, I remember it as if it were yesterday. I ran to Amika the moment I arrived at work and shared my encounter with PaPa. We laughed and cried together and praised Him for my complete healing from this grief!

In quiet times to come, I would ask Him if I had any other sins tucked away in my memories that I had forgotten about. I wanted to make sure I didn't carry another sin for a minute, much less 34 years!

I will forever be grateful to PaPa for trusting Amika with His question. I am deeply grateful to her for her faithfulness in finding the right time to ask me, over and over and over again. I'm also grateful that Amika is not easily offended, as I continued to give her a hard time for asking me this "dumb" question. You see, she knew that she had been trusted by our Heavenly Father to ask a question, a question that would bring about something BIG. She utilized her faith muscles and was not about to give up the walk until she got the "ok" from Him.

Amika ~ I love you

3 John 1:2 "Dear friend, I pray that you may enjoy good health and that all may go well with you, even as your soul is getting along well."

REFLECTING PAGE

- **Take a moment to list the things that you took away from my story. Did anything hit home with you?**

_____

_____

_____

- Ask the Holy Spirit who you can be their "Amika"? In other words, He wants to trust you like He did Amika. He wants you to be a good and trusted friend to someone and ask the question(s) that point them back to our Heavenly Father.

_____

- When is the best time to talk with your friend and ask the tough question?

_____

- Ask the Holy Spirit to prepare you for this time.

_____

Grief Comes In Different Shapes & Sizes

♥

I just wanted to share that as you know, grief comes in different shapes and sizes. Each one of us is affected by grief in one way or another at many times throughout our lifetime. Grief can be long, drawn-out, and exhausting. Yet, there are so many situations when grief is thrown into our personal space at the speed of sound! Thus, leaving one stunned, in shock, and finding it most difficult to breathe. I have found that when I keep my eyes on Jesus, He is ready and willing to walk through it with me. Jesus makes grief so much easier. I mean His peace keeps me centered and I can feel His presence with me, even through the tears of grief.

Grief visits the young teenage girl when she doesn't wear the stylish clothes or name brands that "the popular girls" wear. To adults, it may seem that "grief" is too strong of a word to utilize here, but you need to remember those teenage years. To a teenager, friends and things are more important than family. Not to mention the grief that a young teen feels when she doesn't have any dates, these things matter to the heart of a young girl.

Grief ran over me again six years after my Mother went to be with Jesus when my Daddy passed away after his short battle with cancer. It's the strangest thing to experience when you find yourself not having a parent living anymore. That day left Jan, Chuck, and me knowing that we would see our parents again in Heaven one day.

My family experienced grief when my beautiful 19-year-old niece, Brooks passed away suddenly. As you can imagine, the grief I experienced as her Aunt was much different than that of my brother, Chuck who is her Dad. I can only imagine the intense grief that my brother experienced as he began coping with the reality that his sweet daughter was no longer on this earth. I do know that his heart will be completely healed when he joins Jesus one day.

My sweet great-nephew, Price was only 14 years old when he went home to Jesus. Again, my heart was broken with this grief, and yet the grief that my dear nephew and niece (Bryan and Jana) experienced as his parents was off the charts, to a whole different type of grief pain. The same could be said for Bryana (his sister). I know my sister, Jan (Price's NaNa) would not even have the words to define the grief that she experienced. Grief hits all of us on so many different levels.

Unfortunately, grief hit my family again when my dear nephew, Andy passed away suddenly. I can tell you that my brother is the strongest person I know! He has experienced the death of two of his three children. I can only imagine that the pain of this depth is similar to being hit by a sonic boom – and I'm only guessing. I do know that Chuck relies on Jesus for his strength and comfort.

My dear father-in-law passed away suddenly (twelve years ago). The intense pain caused by this grief left my wonderful husband and me numb! My Mother-in-law and brother-in-law both felt this intense pain in their own ways as well. Both of our daughters were walking through the shock waves of their grief for a season.

My favorite Aunt and Uncle on my Mother's side from Alabama passed away just days after each other and my heart broke. I have great memories of both of them. My heart still hurts for my cousins who have buried both of their parents. I know that they miss them dearly.

Over the last few years, I have experienced the loss of numerous friends while we lived out of state. I can tell you that when each of my close friends went to be with Jesus and I was not able to attend their life celebration, it was difficult for me to understand that they were truly gone from this world. Last week, Steven and I visited our old church office where I worked for 7 years with several of my friends who passed away while we lived out of state. The grief of these friends stood up and hit me in the face and squeezed my heart with such sadness because their absence was very real now! Grief – appears when we least expect it.

Just this week (Sept 2024) a close family friend passed away in a tragic accident and his funeral was yesterday. The ripple effects of grief from his death are surging through his dear wife, family, and friends right now as I add this grief to my book. It just reminds me that we never know when grief will run into us like a freight train!

If you ask me, grief leaves a raw wound when it hits! It's too large of a wound to obtain stitches. It's one of those wounds that a physician would leave open, lightly medicated, and bandaged as it heals. One that will leave a big scar as it heals over the minutes, the hours, the days, the weeks, and the years that follow. As I found myself stumbling through each of these moments of grief in my own life, I cried and spent sleepless nights talking with the Holy Spirit. There were also times when I didn't have the words to express my pain, so my tears did the talking to Jesus for me. I can tell you that Jesus is faithful and held me in His arms, wiping away each tear as I walked through my grief for each one of my family members and friends. I could not have walked through my grief experiences without PaPa! There is just no way! The Holy Spirit is an amazing comforter and I'm forever grateful to Him for never leaving me alone. Especially when being alone is what I thought I needed.

Have you ever had a close friend for a season in your life who was very close, and then they decided to take a random turn in their life that separated your friendship? Although they are still alive, because they are no longer a close friend, it's another form of grief.

Infertility is a grief all on its own! I went through ten years of infertility and I must share that eight of those years were lived in secret. While my friends were becoming parents, I was crying out to PaPa for children. All the while people who meant well asked when we were going to start our family. Grief led us to begin living a lie. My husband (at that time) and I started telling people that we didn't want any children. I would go so far as to say I didn't like kids! GRIEF! Trust me, it could also be called a silent killer because I allowed it into my heart and began living this lie! This lie brought in shame as well. At that time, it was easier to live the lie, than face the truth of wanting a baby so desperately and not getting pregnant. This lie allowed me to grieve and cry in private for almost a decade! Trust me, this is not the time to be alone. We need to let Jesus into our pain of grief. We also need to talk with our closest friend, who will keep our secret and point us back to our Heavenly Father.

While walking through the infertility was the hardest thing I've ever experienced. I do want to share that PaPa brought incredible beauty into my life as a direct result of infertility! We adopted our beautiful daughter, Brooks (she is named after my niece)! ***Isaiah 61:3*** **"and provide for those who grieve in Zion — to bestow on them a crown of beauty instead of ashes, the oil of gladness instead of mourning, and a garment of praise instead of a spirit of despair. They will be called oaks of righteousness, a planting of the Lord for the display of his splendor." (NIV)**

A miscarriage is another grief that words cannot express. I've had an individual very close to me walk through the grief of a miscarriage. I saw what it did to her and it broke my heart! I spent hours talking with PaPa about the pain and an equal amount of time with Him when I could not utter a single word. I know she will see her baby again when she goes to be with Jesus someday and there is sweet joy in knowing this! I am forever grateful to Jesus for holding our hands as she walked through this season in her life.

The death of a fir baby (dog and/or cat) that has been in your life for minutes or 18 years is another form of grief. In 2022 our 18-year-old cat, Maverick passed away. He lived a good and long life, yet it was still hard when he passed. Then a few months later, our Mindy (16-year-old dog) passed away too. Gosh, the house was extremely quiet to both Steven and me.

Grief is a unique raw pain that comes in a variety of ways as we have discussed. I want to encourage you to continue to talk with your Heavenly Father about your feelings. You know, just because we are walking through this pain, does not mean that He is mad at us. Only He knows why this situation happened and that's all I need to know. I don't understand the situation, however; I do understand my PaPa! When I keep my heart soft for Him, it honestly helps me so much! I never want to be mad at him for a moment, much less another 34 years! He owes me no explanation because He is God and I trust Him. He is so caring and loving as He gently walks through the pain of grief with us. Please allow Him to walk with you. I promise He will wrap His love around YOU! **Psalm 5:12 "Lord, how wonderfully you bless the righteous. Your favor wraps around each one and covers them under your canopy of kindness and joy." (TPT)**

In my experience with the grief of a loved one passing away ~ there is no timeframe when I've crossed a "finish line" so to speak. What I mean, is that there has not been a time defined in my life, when the grief was completely gone. Out of nowhere, something will cause me to miss my mother or another family member so much and I will feel the tears returning. So please don't be tough on yourself when you begin to feel sad and miss your loved one. I want to encourage you to hold onto Jesus' hand and allow Him to walk through the grief with you.

Psalm 34:8 "Taste and see that the Lord is good, blessed is the man who takes refuge in him." (TPT)

Lessons Learned the Southern Way

♥

L essons that my mother taught me, I believe are the typical things every Southern Momma wants for her children, such as:

- Honesty is the best policy.

- **ALWAYS** answer my elders with "Yes Ma'am" or "Yes Sir".

- Dust under the dining room table before guests come to eat.

- Be polite at the dinner table.

- At the table, you must put a napkin in your lap, no elbows on the table, one hand in your lap when you're not using it to eat, no slouching, napkin in your chair when you leave the table but are coming back, napkin to the left of your plate if you are finished eating.

- **ALWAYS** say "please" and "thank you".

- **ALWAYS** say "yes" instead of "yeah" or "Yep".

- When a friend comes over, the guest chooses the games and snacks.

- **<u>ALWAYS</u>** send a thank-you note for a gift! A text will not replace the note.

- When I'm a guest in a home, I cannot ask for something to eat. I must wait until it is offered.

- **<u>ALWAYS</u>** walk your guests to the door when they leave.

- Never let on that you've heard Grandmother tell that story before. Be a good listener.

- At a family gathering, allow the elders to go to the front of the buffet line before everyone else.

- Never take a boy into your room to play, even if both of you are 6 years old and you just want to show him your horse collection.

- Never call a boy by phone. He will call you if he wants to talk.

- How to behave in "big church":

  - Eyes forward

  - No running.

  - No talking.

  - No loud whispering.

  - No looking like you want to say something.

- Eyes closed and head bowed during prayer.

- No turning to see who's behind you.

- No kicking the pew in front of you.

- No fidgeting.

- No taking off your Sunday shoes.

- No pointing.

- No rummaging in my mother's purse.

- No chewing gum.

- Do not pass notes.

- Do try and go to the restroom before service begins.

As I reflected upon my childhood for the above lessons, I must share that I giggled. I hope they put a smile on your face too.

REFLECTING PAGE

- Take a moment to list the things that you took away from my story. Did anything hit home with you?

_____

_____

_____

- Talk with the Holy Spirit and tell Him what's on your heart.

_____

_____

_____

About the Author

Leigh Ann is a wife to Steven, is the mother of two young-adult daughters, has two wonderful sons-in-law, and is a Grandmother (AKA, LaLa) to a beautiful toddler: Brooks, Krista, Kyle, Bilal, and River. The people she met abroad while on outreach trips to spread the love of Jesus are very dear to her. She has had the blessing of ministering to children, youth, and adults in Mexico (eight times), Kenya (twice), Haiti, Cambodia, and Lebanon. She stays in touch with many people she meets in each country.

Leigh Ann was born in Atmore, Alabama, and raised in Stuttgart, Arkansas. She remains thankful for her Southern Baptist roots and her devout Christian mother who raised her to love, trust, and serve Jesus. As I walked alongside a friend in her time of grief, I heard the Holy Spirit ask me to write this book about my grief when my mother left this earth and went to live with Jesus.

Leigh Ann is writing more books and loves serving in her local church, in San Antonio, Texas. Leigh Ann and Steven moved to Bulverde, Texas after she retired in 2023, leaving a piece of their heart in Chubbuck, ID. However; Texas brought her the best gift of all, her children live in Bulverde and San Antonio. Her new manager is her

2-year-old granddaughter, River, whom she enjoys babysitting three days weekly. She enjoys road trips with Steven to soak up scenic views and the delightful small-town atmosphere in her community. She and Steven are living their dream with God!

Also by

The book titles that are *italicized* and underlined are specifically designed for teenage young ladies.

All of my books can be purchased from Amazon.

DISCOVERING GOD'S HEART

JOURNEY INTO THE HOLY OF HOLIES

PRAISING THE ONE I LOVE

IN A MINUTE

IN HIS PRESENCE

MY TIME

FAITH STEPS INTO MISSION TRIPS

THE COLORS OF GRACE

LIVING THROUGH THE GRIEF

•

Social Media Information

♥

<u>Please follow me on any or all of my social media platforms.</u>

<u>FACEBOOK ~ LEIGH ANNHAGAMAN PEARSON</u>
<u>FACEBOOK ~ LEIGH ANNPEARSON</u>
<u>INSTAGRAM ~LEIGH_ANN60</u>
<u>INSTAGRAM ~ AUTHORLEIGHANNPEARSON</u>

Made in the USA
Columbia, SC
25 September 2024

42982164R00037